The Pillow Book Of Carol Tinker

The Pillow Book

of

Carol Tinker

FOREWORD BY KENNETH REXROTH

1980
Cadmus Editions Santa Barbara

First published in 1980 by:
Cadmus Editions
Box 4725
Santa Barbara
California 93103

Design of cover ornament by Lindsey Greer;
calligraphy by Ling Chung. Cover
printed and designed by Graham Mackintosh.

Acknowledgments: The Seabury Press & *The American Poetry
Review, Ararat, Four Dogs Mountain Songs, Invisible City, New
Directions Annual* and *Tractor;* the anthologies *For Neruda, For
Chile; Four Young Women;* and *Twenty Times In The Same Place*

Tinker, Carol, 1940 –
LCN 79-57557
ISBN 0-932274-08-0 *(trade edition)*
ISBN 0-932274-09-9 *(signed edition)*

TABLE OF CONTENTS

FOREWORD

by Kenneth Rexroth

Critics somehow seem to have ignored the remarkable fact that, at the peaks and turning points of American poetry, at least since the death of Whitman, there has usually stood a woman. Between his day and the beginning of "modern," that is, populist verse, the leading American poets, Stuart Merrill, Renée Vivien (Pauline Tarn), and Viele-Griffin did not even write in English, but in French, and certainly the most venturesome was Renée Vivien.

With the collapse of Carl Sandburg the best socialist-populist poet was Lola Ridge; H.D. was not only the purest of the Imagists, some people think she was the only Imagist . . . in addition, she invented a free verse based on quantity and cadenced breathing which is still influential; of the five "Classic-Modernists," two were women, Marianne Moore and Mina Loy, and again, both were more venturesome than their male compeers; of the Fugitives group, Laura Riding was far and away the best poet, and when she migrated to London, was the mentor of the young Wystan Auden (when he wrote his best verse); the leading poet of the revolutionary thirties was Muriel Rukeyser; in the post war period Denise Levertov is without question the best poet of the present generation.

So it goes, but few people, even the most passionate feminists, seem to have noticed it. All of these women share a characteristic rare in American poetry: they write in the idiom of international poetry. They are colleagues of Louis Aragon, Paul Éluard, Pierre Reverdy, Gunnar Ekelöf, Paul Celan, Octavio Paz and so on indefinately. This is an international community that few American men poets have been able to penetrate. The women poets I have named are in no case provincials.

Carol Tinker writes in the international idiom and is a voice of a new change in *sensibilité*. She is not a member, much less a leader, of any Movement, although behind her are an indefinite number of seldom published young women who someday may be called a "school." She has published rarely. Whenever she has, her poetry has had maximum impact and influence on those competent to listen. She is inadequately known simply because she has never made any serious attempt to publish her poetry in magazines, although she dominates the anthologies where she has appeared, especially the well-known *Four Young Women*.

Her style represents a new departure because it expresses a new *sensibilité*, a new *weltanschauung*, (to adopt what Henry James called Whitman's "unfortunate familiarity with foreign languages") – but sensibility and world view don't mean exactly the same thing.

What is this new outlook on life? It's not the Neo-Marxism or Neo-Anarchism of most contemporary intellectuals in Europe, although she speaks often in their terms and makes their judgements. She is a poet of the death of capitalism as Kathy Acker is one of its prose poets. However, she does not view the impending collapse of civilization and probable explosion of the planet with horror but with an acid wit. Usually she writes about something more important. There is nothing of Shiraishi Kazuko's sense of being lost in the typhoon of the undamned. A devoted feminist, she has never found it necessary to write poems urging others to "join up" or poems proving the natural superiority of women. The self-evident she always leaves aside.

If poetry is the symbolic criticism of values, the values which survive her criticism are not greatly different from those that withstand the weathering of millénia in *Gilgamesh* and the *Iliad*. What counts is the Grace of erotic comradeship in the night bound world. What endures, as Homer and Théophile Gautier agreed, are "the blithe hexameters" and the chiseled faces of the Greek kings of Bactria, except for their coins, totally lost in the dust of time.

So in an age overwhelmed with mediocrity in poetry and fraud in the plastic arts, Carol Tinker, like most true revolutionaries, is a true conservative.

for Kenneth

I

Calm and struck sails
I want what you want
A calm
Empty days and
Cumulative energy like thought
Forgetting

II

RAKE

The bamboo rake sweeps
In rhythmic patience
The turning of this year
Into autumn
We have connived this
Timing
We have waited full circle
Until now
Waiting for the gold sycamore
Even though light lessens
Long sun rays
Reach, even to us
Who glow enough, bright
With the rake's patience

III

REGATTA

I will move you and
Deliver you as the wind moves
The regatta in high seas to the lip of beach
Raise you as sails are raised and set to the breeze
I will cover you as work covers you
Make images of you, the ringing bells
I will climb above you on the ladders
Of raised heads
I will hold you as my obsession
As parables of naked prey
And I will believe everything about you
As the ones who believe in prayer
And I will
Charter you in that regatta that leans into
The lip of earth

IV

DISSERTATION

Dead white branches on grey
Cypress tree at twilight that
Later becomes night, our night
Sparks from this tinder
Gives glimpses of your face
Your voice speaking to me
Your measured generous voice
Walk carefully on even the clearest path
Speak carefully on the clearest matters
Leave me at night astonished
At night astonished

V

ANGUISH AND FORM AND PRAYER
on the death of my mother

The crimson litter of
Fallen bougainvillea flowers
Drifts across the patio
Where you stand
As though dowsing for water
As though
In another age, as though
Practicing an old and simple
Art to do with
Bringing rain . . . . . . and a cat cries

Or at least I think
I see you stand so, or
Am wishing such
As I raise and turn
My drowsy head, looking
For my reflection in
Your eyes that are now
Closed, looking steadily at
Your icy face among the
Stock
Fixed in encaustic as
Those portraits of ancient
Egyptian and Roman ladies
Once so kind
Now so far away

VI

Is there anything more beautiful
on this earth to regard than the Tessin,
the deep blue clematis of the tea masters

Examining the items of my devotion
From first perception over years of
Apperception and response, from the
Nature of patterns, the dizziness of textures,
Those things, all those other things
That I can now so lose my querulous nudging of
The outside there
In this
Response, in gasping decorum
O aperture on what is
Epiphany and plain open flower

VII

LEGEND

Legend styled catalyst in
The room that is passion
The room as well could be, could include
Trees, includes sky
Inclusion alone, the room that passion
Claims as history and journal
Claiming the claimed, the conceit, the
Shadow love, the small heart's giant holding,
Fully open flower, claiming universal claims
Room as passion, legend as catalyst

VIII

THE ROAD QUEEN

A spectacle of cruelty
A stand of cypress burning
The eyelid drops on no mans land
Hot ashes fall below eye level
To form a mold
Of what is seen
The mold that needs the ear to test it
Ringing true
A bell like form
Studded with rocks that fall like jewels from their setting
As time collapses
A hen scratches
And words echo each other in foreign languages –
Time in the wind tunnel
As the eyelid drops
A pear tree blooms with the dead
Lace curtains blow across pheasant feathers
Textures fight in the surface of stone
The air is thick with the obvious
While going inland with weak eyes
Leaving the sea behind
Gold greys in the fading light
To say time collapses denies Aristotle
To say time collapses denies Herakleitos
Stumbling around stiff legged
To hang a bell on a grave.

On the summit standing burning
Purity of heart says the Iroquois woman who defines
By torture
Purity of heart says the Aztec priest who cuts out the heart
Where we are standing
In a place where the war seems over

Relying on the boredom that hunts for a room of mirrors
To deny its enclosure
The boredom that sweeps the room clean
Of necessary bric a brac
Throws out the dead roses that festoon
The chic coffee shop on Shijodori

Dream works mechanically, gears fall into place
Dream is pegged out like a drying skin
To be worked and reworked by chewing
The nose takes over
And remembers, the nose never meets anything new,
The nose, dog of memory, dreams a pursuit
Of what went this way before

This was a slow world, built by hand
Scavenged and stolen and bought
Burning incense in the hand built world
The censor swinging in the darkness.

IX

THE PUPPET QUEEN

Tunneling through the construct
She said she would build something
As she collects supplies
To construct a construct for
Impulse to tunnel through
Not an impulse for mounting
The one real jewel
That is light from the room of a house at night
Spreading as though over water
The cramped muscle doesn't understand
But the arm tunnels through the air
To make things on strings dance
She said in Japan
I'm particular
But that doesn't mean unique
She is the true scientist who argues with Descartes
Has assimilated Needham as glamour in a dark house
Examines the evidence in the microscope
And prefers to consult a gypsy
Who can explain the Asian man in the teacup
And the cowboy
To an adventuress who never leaves home
Tell me Puppet Queen
Will you marry the sea captain
Divorce the film director
Captivate a bishop
Corrupt a mathematician
Like so many telephone poles
So you can patronize with taste

X

THANK YOU CAPITALISM
FOR THE EXPANDING UNIVERSE

O Tucumcari lady took good care of you
Tucumcari lady made you free
Roast dog and fat tobacco tea

Says
I'm better than a restaurant
Comforted with scalpels, peeling
Off a billboard
Laughing in the stretcher
Happy in the bread machine
        Reclaimed from Greyhound

Pure mind knows
She broke you
Of riots and spreading diseases
So that all your clothes are washed forever
So that you could stand here naked

Cellists!   Miwoks!   Fleas!
Mary pestered by angels!
Hermes nude on washday his finger in the dyke!

It is hard   It is duty

Tucumcari took good care of you
It's just that history
Got you busted

XI

NARAMASU

Hungry, you with
The wish   Come
Reach a form

I chewed wheat
Embers of anomie

The wild grass
            The bamboo grove
The sparrows seethe.

XII

GOLD WIRES
                for Kenneth

I know what you came to say
While you talk to me your heart pulsates
Your breath warms me as our speech makes
A special kind of frost that rimes my body
What shall I answer you
I need your lips against my breasts

              ★   ★   ★

What am I to tell you, alone in the dark
I am quivering in empty space
You are telling me that you are only sadly alone
You who spin and wind and twist the wires
Charged with message
I've come home to a home that is leaving me
That is spinning off into weightless distance
Into the emptiness that is
Full of matter, that
Bombards your fantastically fine and intricate
Nerves and brain
You speak so softly they cannot hear

              ★   ★   ★

The fine hair on your arm brushes mine
And I feel within my chest and belly
Mercury, tiny balls bounce and bound
Fast, heavy and heedless quicksilver
If so slight a touch makes me turn to you open
Smiling, what more do you want
Me lying sleepless, alone

I turn toward you
Can you know what I know

Can I know what you know
Your nerves are older, lead me through
Your nerves, your veins, to your brain
And there in the interstices and convolution
Of loves I have never known, of numbers and series
And interlocking relationships of any resonating
Event that is measurable at all
Lead me through these sequences and I too shall hear
The music of Pythagoras
Of a singing gold wire shaking in
Infinite space

★   ★   ★

And can I tell you, clearly tell you
How long the days are
And how I don't know what they've been or held
The years grow as the grass grows
How can I tell you that the Coast is kind to me
I'm tangled in karma, in the down timber of the soul
The distance is good to us, otherwise you would
Learn things unknowable, that I cannot tell
That you could tell if you touched me
The sea beside us, the knocking tide,
Wildfire across the canyon. Doves are
Cruel, not kind to each other.

★   ★   ★

In this long slow dialogue that begins
The years to come
You tell me that you know that we need to
Know each other
Warm sweet air drifting through swallows and
Facing rocks into an inlet
In this long slow dialogue of years to come

26

Will you remember the beginning
Will you remember when you are râling
In a hospital bed, with the odor of the
Special ointments of the dying folding
You into asphixiation

★   ★   ★

Be careful of me, I can only be wound
Or drawn so far and I will snap
You don't know what lies in my universe
The shiver peculiar to this particular wrist
That shakes a vast fidelity . . . . most, cypress
And monterey pine, the strange atempo waltz of
The eucalyptus on still days . . . .
Be careful, the mirrors show other mirrors
Framed with cracked gilt, with chrome and then at last
With nothing to define their limits
They merge one into the other receding always before you
With aged silver lifting . . . .
Watch out for the cobwebs and the single wolf spider
Once frightened, transfixed, will not move for days . . . .
Or shall I love and cherish the little singing minutes
Listen to me, I am really a conch shell held
To your ears and mouth, that throbbing of the ocean
Is all I can send you . . . . from this my dimension . . . .
My far away lurch in time

★   ★   ★

And so the gold above the years
Crinkles in folds as they surge beneath
So the lime sifts through our bones
Through towers of eroded turquoise to the
Base metal that eventually explodes
Poison runs and washes through filaments of

Iron on the surface, runs downstream
There is a defect in the turquoise
An imperfection filled with tar . . . .
Bituminous marsh of the heart!
Ghostfires of marsh gas in the night of antimony . . . .
My heart crumbles, crumbles, soft rottenstone
Use it to clean your ivory soul
Use it to rub the piano keys

★   ★   ★

Each of those miles I have covered with wanting
And we are each secrets
Each of your secrets challenges mine, each
Of your miles, my miles
Who goes there? Who's that?
I love each perfect, completed mile . . . . . .

★   ★   ★

I come to
You worshipping myself O
Distant lover   the moon
Of late July, rosy and less than
Full   the moon rusted
The oxblood moon firelit, O
Distant lover

28

XIII

Shiva
Is dancing
In the fire
As you turn those pages

As you turn those pages
Fine paper ashes float
Through the room
Your voice goes on

Those marching in the streets
Have fired the garbage on the stairs
And throw flaming papers in the air
Ashes drift and swirl
Around your head

As you turn those pages
Each weft of the cloth
Of your clothes
Holds a
Pulsing
Star

XIV

IN MEMORY OF OTTO RENÉ CASTILLO
POET AND GUERRILLA
BURNED ALIVE, GUATEMALA 1967

No it
Doesn't   run like a
River
No it never
Falls in   rain or in a blinding
Beating leaf tearing storm
No
Nothing like the works of water on rock
Of oceans on granite shores
Of floods forcing debris
Into settlements
No
Lightning begins
The holocaust   in this
Climate burning
Over ground   forcing
Seed
Otherwise the trees
Cannot renew   the chapparal
Will never come back   the earth

Would tear loose in
Avalanches of topsoil eroded
To acid slag
A
Globe of slag
Seared forever
Otto René Castillo

XV

THE PILLOW BOOK

24th of December and a cold rain is falling
A gentle insulated noise overhead
The grey light stationary, permanent
Framing the faded maple leaves
The chill of the room spreads into each corner
One with the grey light and the soft rain
And the bare hedge of naked branches against the sky

★   ★   ★

The resonance of the empty room reminds
You of people who exist
A serious trough in the education
Of the soul
A gully of attachment
To perceive a room as full of ghosts
Forces the mind to people the
Universe with empty gongs

★   ★   ★

Not now, not even now
Does the intelligence require
More information than the flicker of lights
On the road at night
How do I know what I suppose
In the dim light
Flickers of meaning
The dog growling at a passing smell
All day long staring at the bark
Of a thick trunk of maple
Its long and narrow ridges
Seeming real

★   ★   ★

Children fly kites in the Siberian wind
That raises a sandstorm
In the construction yard
Art flowers in imaginary landscapes
Distilled from mind alone
A ragged kite carried to a vast height
By random winds
Dips and dances like an eel

        ★   ★   ★

Drama and disaster of the
Struggling mind seen as natural
As in nature perpetual aggression turns
To anger striking down mists
Churning over the hillside
Eddying inside the garden
Settling, settled
The shortest day fixes the
Intense disagreement of the wind
Like a tic

        ★   ★   ★

To be aware of what
Disturbs the imagination in its
Knitting up of experience
The distracting
Event that costs stitches
In the management of morning
As it comes into our heads

        ★   ★   ★

It is the special light of winter at the solstice
That shines on the wet tile roofs
The notion of which made Sei Shōnagon uneasy

The rose of the sunset streams through the hazy sky
Like through a mirror of damaged silver
Now through the foothills of Kyoto

★ ★ ★

Hard astonishment rocks
The perceiving mind
The web stretched across the window
Shivers with flies
Hanging on nobly to consciousness
The person scatters in the effort of
Concentration
The psyche shrinks and spreads
Rocking in the grey winter light of the mind

★ ★ ★

Waking to pages and more pages
Flickering with a warm wit and a cold tongue
A tired hand that repeats itself
With Buddhist negatives

★ ★ ★

I stand in a blowing wind
In a strange place
The wind blows the sun away
The wind circles the earth

XVI

SWEET MAMA TREE TOP TALL, WON'T YOU KINDLY TURN YOUR DAMPER DOWN

Electric evening with the waterglow of
                    waxy light on the algerian ivy
Beyond through black tree trunks almost white lawn
And true orange lights of broad windows and two fixed
And a third above fixed sparkling
Here in with something intolerant and Texan
And something that shows in sharp movement
Something not polite, not in love but demanding even
    to asking
Even to saying
To a slippery thing that is a later
Quivering as light over a dull aluminum sheet reflector
Preludes to this
This is my mind   this is my mind now
That this I fear when doing in the future
You in listening as to a curiosity
While I'm doing in the future
It must be certain sure and able
It must be warm and a guide
It must smile and ask and then
When I am supposed to glow
The fire encourages the reaching

XVII

REMEMBERER

I'm the rememberer
My watching eyes tell you you've forgotten something
What's written about it is over your head
Full of private references partially painted over
What's more, the characters are illegible
So there's no guide to what's left over
You've got to deduce the rationale of the society
From its tangible relics
The army and baggage train flowed like the Yang-tse Kiang
Carrying silt
A river rolling to the sea slows in its delta

XVIII

STRONG LIGHT

This morning's high blue skies, bluer than blue
And the white trunks of the young eucalyptus in a
Slight palsy
Of snarls of tints of silver, yellow green
Superimposed another raft of leaves in shadow
        not from clouds
But from other higher branches
Out into the light, drag it out
Spread it on the ground to dry or use it to signal in the air
That shimmers as the pointilistes' perception
And drag it out, to deal alone with perception
I am not emerging from Plato's cave
But I am as if coming out of an ancient Quaker house,
        from the
Secret room built for the Underground Railway
From a house where most rooms are built on different levels
And the lawn pushes up bullets from the Civil War
At the starkness, the simplicity of strong light
At the simplicity and complexity of the articulation
        of natural objects
At night in the moon yin yang seen, rocking as though
A basket on a Ferris wheel
Bewildered at the slightest rocking motion
It is this process as if emerging from a crysalis
As a place to hide in the face of certain death
That I perceive human emotions as natural objects
And that I perceive myself as one, alterable by chemical
Chance due to stress of weather and of humankind
And that the simply perceived rock wall face
Provokes no emotion but perception of a permanent
        chemical change in the brain
In this new light, myself, casting a shadow, knows
What I can see and feel – knows a personal transformation

Into an American kind of Kali, the fugitive slave, the
Native American mother, the Quaker theatre where this
      takes place
The absoluteness of feminine responsibility understood
Only as threat, as guilt. So situated I can see
The hermit thrush landing injured close at hand
I will not touch you, hermit thrush, with my clumsy
Sympathy, as you drag your wing

XIX

ANOTHER DEFENESTRATION IN PRAGUE
for Fernando Alegría

At Mireya's beach house
We are friends, we are eating flan
We are discussing the people killed in Chile
We are talking about technology
We are discussing international control of finance
We are describing The United States

We stare hopefully at each other
    Out of our own hopelessness
The blood is too recent
Telephones:
         "How is Raphael?" "Raphael is very well"
         "How is Susanna?" "Susanna is sick"
         "How is Manuel?" "Manuel is very ill"
         "How is . . . .

I do not have the habits of power
I don't know how to use these telephones
The corpses are too new

XX
LANK PIER

Partially
Off course the moment rises
Part ebbs
Reflects at the lank pier
Sags below the surface
Tension
Far too much too taut
Sight it
Put a beyond
A *cimaise*

Set up
A decision approach
Slowly
Regard

The inventory round the
Many axes many
Decisions then
Contemplate a vanishing
Point a topological
Change the left
Hand come upon the
Method juxtaposition

A monopoly an
Image cluster of such
Pith that any way you throw
The jackstraws of

Changing light
At the change of axis
Where tension slacks a
Cosmos immanent
Set up a
Decision
At the lank pier

XXI

STRUCTURE

To prefer the structure
Is to prefer the thief
Never demonstrably brave or flying
But enduring alone in her house
Constructed of abstractions such as
War and Death and Structure
Everything in life seen as a kind of murder
The decor is economic
The epoch making works are
An abyss for financing
Elegant solutions
The real stands shivering as a file clerk
Afraid of losing her job
This is not the picture of an old woman
This is cultivation

XXII

Thank you for your
Birthday
            all the
Time we tithe
                    and here
On this earth
                        no one
Is ungrateful for a meal

                    and
Memories
            as expensive as
Ambiguous friends
                        have come
To tell stories
                to go away

And surely these
People
        never forget
                    what bites
But people
            forget
                plenty of sadness

Thank you for your
Birthday
            the lights
                        the throng
That
        glance and turn
                    turn and glance

42

XXIII

POEM BEGINNING THIEF

Person who stole
Landlady's wash left her
Without panties stocking bathtowels
Her blue housedress is gone too

Must have been poor and ornery
And her size

Fine yachts in the harbor
Make a difference between
The law of inventory
And the right to
Lynch

    This is not a quiet night
    Guns and sirens and running feet
    Screeching tires screams
    Breaking glass and more shots, this
    Time an automatic rifle

Read this for its sentiment
Differentiating lynch law from
The right to inventory

XXIV

SHOVE DAY

Like the human measured in Leonardo's drawing
Describing a circle
We stretch and span each other, matching
Reaching, not to wrestle but for aid and comfort
It is solace indeed
It is our devotion to Avalokitshvara
Bending from the waists, the arabesque, the support
Naked, nonchalant,
Two hands touch
And again two hands do not touch
Two hands dream of consolation
Two hands reaching as at rest, this compassion

XXV

Carbuncle of blind
And murderous heads the
Patriarch and his murdering
Sons hunted
Gnats and brush whipping his eyes
On the sunlit forest floor

All queens and their
Uncles under the
Ribcage shattered blow by
Blow
        The hollowed heart eaten
Hollowed out of causes, wept and eaten

Poker flays
The streets   Fireworks
Boil above

Further out on the pier
Two older more naked
Lovers
Talk
Louder softer warmer

XXVI

LAURA ULEWICZ

O Laura
Laura
     circled round
With loves and
Lovers
      she
Is bound to
Bees
    to
Lovers and to
        flowers

XXVII

AT THE CLOSE OF A FILM ON NATIVE
AMERICAN WARS I REQUEST A NEW MOVIE
OF CHINGHIS KHAN

Dickering in
The market place   do we
See the style I stop to
Note
     the faces facing backwards
The motion retrograde
The elements of action analysed
Resynthesized, latching
Onto a vision of face and face alone, knuckles
White with strain
               a motif
Where there are no motifs but
Gantries to lift a satellite to the moon
Inconclusive logic
A bangle of shell from Thailand
Knocks against a bangle of copper: this syllogism
The anthropological blundering through neighbors' gardens
In isolating value –

Passion and input untie to propel
Emptyheaded road queen bicycling through a
Tunnel with impaired vertical clearance
Sade in his brittle raincoat flashing
Now you see it, now you don't
The luxurious panoply of the Threefold Lotus Sutra
The end use of the lever
So play I'm the reiterating polo player
Out of India with cauliflower ears
Standing in the stirrups
I save you the trouble of closing the circle of the hunt

XXVIII
DEATH RATTLE

Closing the eyelids
Follow in the path of the dry river

XXIX

NATIVE SONG AND INVOCATION

Secret mountain
Secret mountain
A man in trouble

XXX

THE ART OF POETRY

Simple words, wonderful frogs –
Measure, then molest each expression
You can lay hands on.

XXXI
CARESS

Thus caressing my moodiness as if smoothing gold leaf
Or blind, I run my fingers across the tessarae of events
Intent on the varying levels of Theodora's portrait
Finding the events crowded at dense intervals
With the repartée of fingers
A sensuous mysticism, a mysticism of weaving
Gives over to a hard, Cavafy-like wistfulness
That only fondles the ivory of those who've died
In these encounters
Stranded in strange cities and
Run over by chic friends
With mutual respiration, a suave emotion,
The verbal caress transforming cherished and destroyed
Bodies into marble
Or at the least into the glass and metal forms of
The disfigured present that plummet into the ocean like
Zinc weights measuring the depth of the Pacific
Something breaks, cracks, sparks, shorts, disconnects
In the relentless obtrusiveness
Of exact circumstance –
While a telephone call from far away
Resembles the immediate taste of lips grazing lips,
I dismiss these exactions, becoming an amnesiac
But still parenthetically abused by this circumstance
This rubber mallet that imperceptably mauls
The bruises a memory sequestered to mature like burgundy
Then again, a sensation like a burn, while holding
The telephone receiver that connects to nothing –
As though I've been slashed by a razor in the city
Feeling nothing at the time but only seeing
Someone running by flashing metal.

XXXII

A RAG, A BONE AND A HANK OF HAIR

Koto music on the phonograph
The moon is full and I am restless
Full of illusion, infatuated by dreams,
Moved by your desire

A month ago a red moon over the pines
Tonight pale, in another kind of pine
Pale, lost, drifting across black branches

Drifting. Lost ponies, O questions
The sea seems saltier now than then
A rag on a stick, a hank of hair
Snyder as Villon, crying *d'antan!*
Laura in the blossoms –

       You must not! Must not! Must!

"these poems, people,
         lost ponies with
Dragging saddles . . . . . "

           The one needs the other,
           The refraction, the reciprocal
           The whirling indifference of stars

I feed on lotus
I feed in the stumbling surf, I look
For lost ponies
As I trace your shoulder with my tongue

           "the ache of knowing you're gone"

XXXIII

The tissue sent with
Vision the integrity of
Carcinoma of tons of flesh
Of bones of bellies nail parings
Roasting in an ashtray

Here's a dog
Drill down
Unconnected sound sending
    The frets go dark
        Goldbeater's membrane

Through which
    He's standing talking not me

Die two at a time arbutus
Smell it   a white noon
Assimilate the female principle
Not a
Love story

XXXIV

GOLDEN TRIANGLE

I was a saint
Went up in a
Basket
Seventy times as high
As the moon

"I saw Pittsburgh
I saw town
I saw Allegheny   upside down"

      Saw eighty million working women
      Ride red hot motorcycles
      Saw many many women
      Working all the time

Saw some woman
Eating breakfast at sunset

Saw one hat
On the precise, teak

      (many, many)

Hooks.

XXXV

THE ANGLE OF INCIDENCE IS EQUAL TO THE ANGLE OF REPOSE

I remember the
Sweetness
I knew that
Hand but
Now in the false
World of real

Hands the sweetness
Passes
Into sound

XXXVI
SILENCE

With a black rock sated
A black confession done
A weariness of the white of twisting branches
And the mealtimes that linger into other mealtimes
Now the glass cracks in the pattern of sun rays
                around the bullet hole
Into the bright cave's heart of diners
With the aloes, with the agave, with tropical italics
With the ticking of hot metal as it cools off
With the dream enchantment by dream lovers
And the perplexed silent neutrality of the physician

With the various systems of nerves arguing the pluperfect
Against the authority of a hand imperiously raised to signal
A shadow ridden desolation of cement blocks
In the fierce tension of a single human hair
A process begins, a history of silence

XXXVII

THE GREAT CHAIN OF BEING

Things simple, and never simple
As though it's a matter of stripping wood
And wire brushing out the grain
A nature with no finish
The tension that manages treasures
Winds a cocoon around time
In each thing loving
A drift of gypsum
Of those in the deep past, for those
Ancestors that
Had a mission
And craved to be stunned by the face of the
God in some not so simple outlander
And so turned from striking Rome
Feet in soft shoes now walk on brambles
Sharp points on the mind's map, the
Memory of burnt cabins
The racial hammerlock

XXXVIII

BUDDHA'S BIRTHDAY
    IN MEMORY OF MARTIN LUTHER KING, JR.

Come & see   you
Have shown me
Passion

Wind blows the eucalyptus
And sun shines through
In Golden Gate Park
Prime among others
                my moving eye

April the fourth month
New spring gardens:
Dogwood flowers on lower Market Street

Buddha's birthday

Requiem mass for Brother Martin
We circumambulate the cathedral and the
                      Pacific Union Club

Passover
      Easter

Or in the Revelation of John:

Nevertheless I have somewhat against thee
Because thou hast left thy first love

The venerable Bede
Knew of the wolf
Taught his paternoster
By monks
All the wolf could say
Was lamb,
                    lamb

XXXIX

TACTICS

Target or spectacle
Aimed at or viewed
It seems an audience is presumed
But
Neither failing nor
Posthumously a question of failing
If this is being, wait around a while

XL

ANIMAL GONE

for Ching, Labrador Alsatian,
poisoned at six years, 1978

Animal removed and shed, shed
You saw the hand bleeds its knowledge
Of curve of bone, of breastbone, ribcage
The hand did its cherishing, in totality
The devotion down the haunch a full curve
Of the coat, this past
Devotion
Now, the trace, the prodding, the desire
Is still a desire to worship, to love
The desire to remember in homage
To praise

XLI

I swear they are all beautiful:
Every one that sleeps is beautiful – everything
* in the dim light is beautiful,*
The wildest and bloodiest is over, and all is peace.

from "The Sleepers" by Walt Whitman

In terrible grief
"I see the clear waters of Lake Tahoe"
Air clamourous with birds
Rushing together
It waits
It is overdue and a long time coming
Belly up
            Between the leads, between the tessarae
Its own defiance
        I do not think it is in the bone
        But in the ligaments along the bone
Its own defiance has served
Custom, labored to
Give us this day
They burned their homes behind them
The most noble and richest was X
Led on by desire for power conspired with the nobility
And persuaded the citizens to leave home well supplied
Prodigious   mutable   floating
Ensemble
In terrible grief
In the dim light beautiful

XLII

SPLINTER

I see through to nothing but
A grey board marked with white paint
With a swiftly crayoned black circle.
Is the day, the hour, news?
Is the splinter you worry under your skin India?
And persons falling out of towers
And this personal dust cloud –
I saw another, I saw a soul
Lightly inscribed on exterior bone
In maturity
I saw it and scraped the bone, scraped like a surgeon,
Working, removing a character, dry.

XLIII

I'm speaking to you of a skyline of hope
Square flag the color of mystery
Negligent cypress of articulation
I'm speaking to you
 The monsoon of the corruption of a mind
Holding no value
I'm speaking to you of the light ribbons lining out
                              the sources of desire
Purchasers of requiem
The breadline of the cogent
The cullers of vision
The speakers of one syllable that seek purity
Of the great premonition, wildfire of the modest
                              and remote

XLIV

THE HESITATION KAMI

Again, *da capo,* from
The top, a crane, a stone
Wind billowing the pine and eucalyptus
This frolic
Because it and my nerves
Billow, as if hair from a heddle stiffened
In skeins settling brocaded
Yet unwoven
So surge in random and absolute frequencies
As the light goes, this early evening the winds
Provide me with scintillation of sea sky in motion
Of the great emu eucalyptus
Then one is ready, what does the one know
Energy surges and fades, things authentic
Appear too powerful, robbing nature
The kami that will finally hesitate
And now the rimless drum, the steady flogging of
The wind at the other side of hesitation.

XLV

I SEE YOU IN BLACK LEATHER

Trashed by words
In hand and body motion
Say nothing and
Say it low

XLVI

ONE BRIDGE OF KÖNIGSBERG

The saints have in fever
Made zero on this
Bridge
That has in mind a maintenance
Of its own curve
The observance of the bow
The saints have studied and
Completed
Saints akimbo or distressed
Arching over water
Specified the only specification.
The saints have forever
Made zero on this bridge.

XLVII

A thousand miles not a single
Stoplight no books a slow
Disentanglement of weeds

Rain on the roof
A thousand heavy dancing crows

A high ditched road through fields of milo

A thousand miles and no stoplight
Rain raining so hard and so often

This layer of atmosphere close to the ground
Is water, a lucid fog
And the small leaves of the live oak,
Cotoneaster, acacia, mimosa
Shine with a wet shine
And move with the motion
Of a thousand miles
A thousand crows

XLVIII

Asking more from landscape
Than from life itself
Be sure to tell the next part of the story
After all this is an international issue

Asking more from landscape
Than from life itself
I wandered through the Japanese countryside
Looking for categories:
Human memory

Mine is of the bamboo groves
Of 1948

All I knew was the story
Of Suzume-san
The tongue cut sparrow
And I hoped to see the
Sparrow world
In glorious kimono

I've heard a poem
By a man named Tanikawa
When he traveled through
Arizona
He questioned if it had any meaning,
If all it was to him
Was scenery
A sentimental idea
How could he see blood on the landscape
Or do you have to be native to feel the rising ghosts
Tanikawa wrote about Billy the Kid, not the otherness
Of the landscape,
The pure otherness of scenery

XLIX

A SMART & FINAL IRIS

Sound rising
Acquires a
Musical structure

Light falls off
By squares

      Love is death
      Feed the hungry ghost

      Here is meet and
      Fitting female
      Here is flint
      Harder than steel

There are celebrities
That are just like you
And just like me
And just like Marsden Hartley
At the second German Sound Shift
At the
      Smart & Final
               Iris Company
Cash & Carry Wholesale Grocery

      There searched according
      To
      Custom they
      Said

GRAVELLY LAKE PONDERS!
    or:
           Relax sweetie you're not going anywhere

STOP CASTING POROSITY!
    or:
           Stick with me baby
           We'll see your name in lights

L

Oceans and stars
Manifest in the cricket turning in
Search on the spine of a book
Each time the cat washes her face I wonder
How many times all the cats that ever lived had
Done the same,
What is the number
The cricket disappears, has gone elsewhere
Relinquishing its search or not, perhaps
Distracted
Distractability liveliness's homage to number
Why is there more than one of any thing
Is there ever more than one of any thing
And what is anything if not one dematrixed
There is no measure of waves but in stolid atoms
An end and a beginning for vibrations
The autonomous one is chaos
Our number the space between events rather than events
The water that doesn't wave, that is always still

LI

MUDRA: A BUDDING LOTUS

for my new niece Caroline Elizabeth

A face on a field of flowers
Eyes following right in fascination
Holding in her own two hands
Reality and its expression,
The opening of a budding lotus!

LII

CATULLUS, STOP LEAVING ME ALONE

The children playing Bartok –
The fundamental notes
Of the *Microcosmos*
Skew my anxious fingers
My rigid shoulder blades
My swollen eyes and fevered palms
O my caged and silent lover, call
Catullus – have him lift his
Still smarting
Elegant hand
Blistered and bankrupt of silver
O call Catullus
To use his special talent on your
Transformation
He will touch his finger tips
With sandpaper
And his twiddling fingers can
Pick the lock
He can crack the safe
Listening to the tumblers
And he'll say those things
Drawn out of a long slow orgasm
That will unwind you
Into a luscious enclosure . . . . .
. . . . can you love
Chaste and narrow shadows
So desperately that
I shall find you at last
Cold, frozen in a corner
A parrot frightened to death
At the glimpse of a mastiff

LIII

HANGOVER

Out of the emptiness volcanic
Ash blackens the hair
Like a brutal hangover in a
Mining camp
The only motive for action is
The same old feudal relation –
Can these things turn into doors?
"I had no worries then
None at all
For everything was taken care of"
Said the former Japanese soldier
Of his career in China
The
Ultimate proving ground of an
Ideology is the prison system –
Who do you jail for what?

LIV

Contemplation as two jade
Fish
Stable, there, steady as
Question
As no question is steady

LV

Full of
Summer pie when the
Hot knife cuts the swing into
Spacelessness
Out gush falling wires

At a bend in the
Test tube, caught on
The meniscus, axle of the wheel
Rolls over me,
                    it's ice
It's feeling goats and fires
On the fringed trees of the
Chasm, roots above and
Limbs below
A real axle of the axis

Two to the right and two left

Flames on the Erechtheum
On the tenacles
On the elevations
On the measure of the house
On the lapse of the steeple
On the coming of the white center
That is the politics of the last hour

Stomach to the ground
Gut under cover
On this
            twisted plane the axis
Moves
            I'm not
Clever in this
                twisting history

LVI

      After the natives
Leave, the heart is
Written out
In pictographs within
The cave's line of sediment
What is written down is
Over   what is
Pictured, the soul is sized
It is not meaning
But meant
Recording their going
And the heart written
Out goes through scene and frame
Strung out lasciviously along
A protected bed
When the natives left
This heart flicks after them
As a quick whiplash
As the touch of a
Scenting snake tongue

LVII

YOU ARE DEAR, NATHANIEL TARN
on his 1978 reading in Santa Barbara

You have left me deeply touched and gratified
But you are so fast and I can't even
Get a good look or impression of
Most birds unless they light
But, Lord, yes, I love the flash

LVIII

CONSEQUENCES

Consequences are margins in
The charged atmosphere that you must
Cover and cross.   A mind
Replete with consequence, a body paid out
Its debtors grounded
Graceful enough yet to
Slip from level to level, from edge to edge
And liquify
The motion and the will
Perhaps are something new

LIX

SANDWICH

Running through the
Rubble of fire bombs and nuclear war
She becomes her own pimp
Everything she does is designed to entice you
Paying for her glasses of water
She doesn't drink to
Injure the merchandise
She's as expensive as possible
Because she takes time and
Dresses it up
And makes it strut through
The rubble
She takes time to make it pay
You only risk what it costs
Each moment is bittersweet
So each moment has a price
This is my sandwich she says
I live off calories
From the great heat

LX

THE PIEBALD POSSUM

Possum, back to me
Glances back and
Freezes, light switched on

So here, pink and black tail
Muzzle black and pink
Coat whitish through black,
Brush dragged out on this paper

As though we froze
On sight
          The things around stricken with light
That out there surprising but not yet anyway
Terror
No threat gape from possum
No death pretense
Guard hairs unalerted
Bravado as climax
And stasis

LXI

DREAMERS

Where dreamers' serious bodies
In lockstep in ceaseless solicitation on beaches
While leafing through gilt edged pages
Hauling ass to known simplicity
Leaving out in every other line
The jungles swarming this nicotine government
Dear dreamers
Dead to any wave
Flat, sighing, drift
On your own reflection

LXII

FOR THOMAS ADLER

Dear friend and helpful mover of goods
This hand hurts, that writes, that's attached
To this body and this sad head
You draw plans, I draw plans,
You form your letters,
Quotas, daybooks, waves,
Dear friend with magazines and
This ongoing talk of film scripts –
Dear friend with magazines.

LXIII

CONSORTS

Lecherous consorts of the low
Afternoon sun, the shadows of bush and tree
Overtaken by tree shade,
The host the sun glancing through
My heart is given to happiness
In light or in parasitic eventime
My heart is given

LXIV

PICK UP

Rome did not have zero
Zero came to us by way of Islam and India,
And after the Mongol or Tatar enthroned on a hill of skulls,
And after your dream of riding with the Golden Horde,
And after attibuting it all, all downcast distorted India
Or the, if I understood you, the corruption of perfection
That is simple moral decline,
And how it's going to come again,
And the civilizations destroyed and the outer cultures
Likewise destroyed,
And there is no more Aryan power,
But time to disembark from the plane.
I picked up a popular magazine and saw your likeness,
Thomas Huxley.

LXV

Give me dread
A road dry, loose pebbles, dirt in shoe
Hot and this is a going somewhere else, being
Heavy in knowing this passage.

What I am breathing, I tell you, you will like
I tell you
This emergency, this emergency by no means overboard,
Crying cancer, crying blunder
Studying the sea they call studying theology
And I tell you all
If the words describe sickness
Ride with the affliction
As in cancers, so in stars

LXVI

COMPOSURE

It pleases me, this grieving
The world, all of it above moving water,
Plowed, harrowed by the fingers
Everlastingly tired old talkers of
Their time in prison

So a day to compose
There she intimidates in turning pages
There is a mine with galleries fish swim through
And an exploded channel
Yet the motive is simple
As all of us together in a
Viennese drawing room of 1913
With the books and the pictures
The sweets, the mood
And this the gauntlet

LXVII

THE WELL FIELD
for Kenneth

The mind's space in body doubled in
Use to singleness
As the web of nerves covers the muscles and
Ligaments of the face under the skin
The well field its nine sections covered with
This webbery of bowstrings
Tuned and plucked
Silk spun as the web of a ground spider
No fear in music in the Dorian mode indicates
Compassion at rest
Evenly regarding the wake of the ship and
The ship's given position
The peach unpeeling, peeled and still entire

My mind reaches for your mind, reaches past
The matching to the
Pentagons read on the flats of our hands
To the thrum of doves safely out of range

Is love a given position on a grid
Where the hairs cross in the gunsight
A point on a line, established by calculation
The focused upon, reticulated
Unseeded chain of questions –
Nets under fruit trees
Net under the walker on wires
Then an act occurs
That is its own net

2

As water before the dry season
A plethora of words
If heard as speech rises
Above the road machinery, planes
Birdsong
My attention diverted yet
The ear backspaces, the road narrows to one lane
The runners and bicycles shunted to one side
In this model
Incidents that flicker over skin
Incite the mind snatcher

3

To arc
To electrically section a cone
At the same time in clear view
The day warming up discards economy
The circle squaring out
Woven so dispassionately as
Life handed down as though
It were chance
But still handed
These hands thrust open into the waterfall

4

Illusion
Springs from the mind
Thus the mind
Acting
Nowhere
Becomes here

LXVIII

HELLENES: IN THE OLD PALACE

Stuffy old room, stuffy old place
Those old women, mothers or not
Hold their blank faces and when
They speak talk of nothing
But the horror
Outside and rarely of their own
Very private enameled interiors
And lay their soft illumined
Hands upon their laps
Graven evenly, the throb of hysteria subsided
But bitter, bitter as the olive, bitter as gall
Seen life enough, seen too much life, will still
Still see more
The mouth draws down at the corners at times
At times it's always thus
But blank blank the faces looking at you
Death expertly shuffled across the floor

LXIX

NUCLEUS

A last presentiment of
Self, half physician, half the sceptic
Archer
Artemis her arrows Artemis her tree
The scholar occluded; the balmy moon curled upon
Itself as the new and blistered almond leaf
And what takes place under this justice sky
Lapsing and thriving, the raucous
Transformation from stone to root to flower
Artemis her embayment
Under March
The physician self with wisdom in the lap
Swells and subsides; the archer in covert
Intent, precise
That justice heaven
And below the forcing of the law
The pale cold release of the mainspring of time
This is the clock now coming apart
This is the measure tripped fantastic
This is the spiral unwinding sweeping
Thriving and thrusting and resting and passing
This is the clock spreading a swath across
What is under justice
A nausea, Artemis, a nausea that is a nebula

LXX

LIGHT

Light sections the
Brigade, the toxic snow
The delicate bitch that come
So stereotyped in dream,
Light cruising over the waiting
Heads, lifting skirts
Or a passing stapled glance
Light cruises over
Brick pillars, onyx glass and the
Striated sound of crystal
Fragmenting into snow
To listen is to deal from shame
To ignore is the punishment of a new shudder

LXXI

"AN UNDEVOUT ASTRONOMER IS MAD"

– Edward Young

Drenching mist the moon
And curious insects
Too early for Purcell
Too late for Bach
This is all complementary
It comes on the house
Synthetic as in synthesis
The mad and undevout astronomer
Who ignores the moon
Who takes one by the hand in
Deep seriousness
To an open book
Frivolity the executive admonishment
Take hold, a song and a meditation,
Flower crowded double talk
Rises to the full moon in tree and mist

LXXII

SHAKEDOWN

for the mime and director R. G. Davis,
being an extended corollary to conversation on narration

Beat the time, the pain, the story
Compose, direct
Like Mykenai a world deformed
Like Pythagoras time as music metered
To the truss of an absolute
Out of the arbitrary
And identity invites the
Mirror thief, all mirrors snatched away
Left to modulate to a lower register
A different key
The snake doctor swoops, snatches, hovers
Thought hitching the wind pulse
The snake doctor all eyes dramaturge
Takes in
The scene
Provokes complicity and complication
Then convection
As high style decanted
Through cultural barriers
Back to back and belly to belly

Downstream the great river
Snake doctor darts over summer foam
A shakedown
Empty your pockets toss over the keys
Take off your clothes
As hands quaver over you
Stand still
To gain the attention of the
Mind vacant with purpose
Mind native and over sophisticated

95

Of the shortest time of history or ocean
Radical scepticism or
The urbane sceptic converts
In the small small places across the sea

Sorting the thread of narrative, a hard business
Snake doctor, you dandy, arcanum
All eyes all hunger
Snake doctor prism maker
Bring your belly down
Teasing the time, the pain, the story
Strand by strand out of Mykenai the knot
Like gnats from the air
Make us hallucinate shock absorbers
Retreat, romantic, back to the imagination wall
Sold on our own susceptibility
Load up on plastiques
Balance on the nail of someone's crucifixion
While courage is that fish limp on the lowest rung of
The ladder
And the box of cartridges in structure perfect ends
Our story, told to death, but unprovable

LXXIII

VELVET

Having nothing to do with me
Yet that hand rests in the pile of velvet sanctions
Comforted, consoled
No one argues with these sanctions
No one cries from pole to pole of
Desolation, moribund,
This upkeep of rinds from fatter times
This tribulation lays like light snow
Over goodly fields, yet unsatisfied
Land occupied by sanctions
That it's not all right
Is the comforting news
Velvet pile or skin to write upon
The sheen
Do not annotate

The tasting of plums
Do not comment on

Free hydrogen atoms
Do not describe

Buddhist bootleggers
Suppliers to ancient patient mind
You think, therefore you think

LXXIV

Pick a love, goes O in the face
Goes O in the face
O if combustible
Is the what that's coming to be
O, so we roast, O sit 'til time
Stays outside the door
O custody O bless
O still O presentable
I would have had a toad
A cast iron toad
Still frozen place still tight eyes
I saw I saw my caricature
The strangest woman ever seen
All this long past a far place some town
A once bricked road above a famous reach of water
If so I fend to give you configuration in wild advice
If so I am levelling
I am for you sand

LXXV

STAKEOUT

Trace elements
So what, so where
The helicopter thrumming over the snail
The end of a silver train
Some tracking, grease of body
Familiar glands
The sidewinder scents and registers heat
But the crucible tips and pours
The struggle within the circle ends
With old sun, young moon,
The mirror, all catcher, guest and householder
Slaked
Quicksilver pilling downstream to
The dragon waters, the rain butlers
But traces are left behind

Blue, blues and wind over blue sky
A drifting malevolence ropes in
The telephones and lets them ring on
At sunrise, and steps follow the ringing until
It stops
Steps to write it down
An icy intelligence
Sidewinder sliding through heavy seeded grass
Boot heel scraping after
Dead trees' antlers hung with ghost fruit
The ledger of partial entries
These spring-in-autumn flowers
Blue, so blue
Human forms of grey felt muffle
Negotiation over the use of charm
The glamour of obsidian knives
In the race to the eye's twilight

Outdistancing great malevolence
The perimeter shrinks as the iris of the eye
Vibrant with hate, lurking with scapegoat
Children, their mariachi minds

Sidewinder, bright, made savage by vision
Crouch then leap
In a paroxysm challenging what stands
For money
Cattle country rider
Horsing around
Lopes slow but sudden
For still dreamers at the bottom of the lake
The ripples from a drinking horse
Beseige their somnolence
And they stir slowly
With birds' plumage and hawks' eyes
Wet bird heads weave a little as fish weave
Encapsulated, will drift away
Those in the upper air
Leave, thinking to build
Unblessed, unappeased

The flat articulation on a piece of paper,
Teeth chattering out a line
Fingers grasping for elegant style
Marked and maculate his defiance
Wrapped in a horn of feathers
A downdrift
Bind bound bonds
As frescoed walls on an alluvial fan
Bind, bound, bonded

The needle here never stops moving
In the territory of hunches
An arm for support is steadier
Than this ground, but armless
The wind dances with disks of moon and sun
And shaman's drum whipped far away

This is a young poem come of age
In vicious times, taking thought to remember
Gentleness
Wind over custom's staked out lake
Still body whipped to provincial fury
Thrashing its shores
Small craft broken on rocks
Would have been safer in the open sea

NOTES

page 20   *The Road Queen* was the name of a boat equipped
          by a wealthy woman to sail around the world at
          the end of the last century.

          Shijodori: The main street of Kyoto.

page 24   *Naramasu:* near Tokyo where I lived as a child.

page 44   *Shove Day:* A mythical day in the United States
          when Negroes are thought to shove Caucasians.

page 65   *Kami:* in Japanese hallowed, sacred, divine, a
          diety.

page 70   *The Smart and Final Iris Company Cash and Carry
          Wholesale Grocery:* a business in Santa Barbara.

          Gravelly Lake Ponders: a highway sign near Port-
          land, Oregon.

          Stop Casting Porosity appears on top of a building
          near Livermore, California.

page 89   *Well field:* The Chinese character *ching,* 井
          "well," is usually used alone for "well field," a
          piece of land divided in nine pieces and culti-
          vated by eight families. The center square was
          taken for taxes.

page 95   *Mykenai:* The House of Atreus.

          Snake doctor: Southern name for the dragonfly,
          supposedly doctors water snakes.

Carol Tinker was born in 1940 in Pittsburgh, Pennsyl-
vania, one of three children. She grew up in New York
City, Japan, and Brandywine Hundred, Delaware. She
attended Carnegie Mellon University, and migrated to San
Francisco in 1962. In 1967-68 she lived in Berlin for six
months and then traveled around the world, and in 1974 she
married the poet Kenneth Rexroth, after a long association.
She has lived in Japan four times – 1947-48, 1968,
1974-75 and 1978. She is a painter as well as a poet and has
lived in Santa Barbara, California since 1968.

This first edition of
THE PILLOW BOOK OF CAROL TINKER
consists of a trade edition in wrappers,
100 copies signed by the poet and the author of the foreword,
& 26 lettered copies.
Signed copies have been sewn and bound by hand
at the Earle Gray bindery.
Typeset in Bembo and Baskerville by Opie Ostrow
at the West Coast Print Center
and printed by Kimberly Press
for Cadmus Editions.